The Ganges

The Ganges

Text and 123 colour photographs by
RAGHUBIR SINGH

THAMES AND HUDSON

To My Mother

Acknowledgments

I would like to thank R.V. Pandit for publishing my first book – *Ganga, Sacred River of India* – in 1974; Nirad C. Chandhari for pointing to the true protagonists of India's life: the mountain, the river and the plain; and Satyajit Ray for introducing me to Nimtita. I would also like to acknowledge the invaluable help of the Maharaja of Banaras, Dr Milo Beach, Ramesh Bhattacharjee, Dean Brown, the Port Commissioners – Calcutta, W.E. Garrett, the late William Gedney, R.P. Gupta, Swami Hansanandji, Anne de Henning, Ruth Keshishian, Dr Rai Anand Krishna, Joseph and Caroline Lelyveld, Glenn and Susan Lowry, J. Anthony Lukas, Mahant Vir Bhadra Mishra, Dr Partha Mitter, Bruce Paulling, John Putman, Ram Rahman, Radhika Rawlley, Aveek Sarkar, Sydney Schanberg, James Shepherd, Asha Sheth, Ketaki Sheth, Vasant Sheth, S.K. Singh, V.P. Singh and V.C. Tiwari.

Note to readers: Throughout this book the Ganges is referred to by the name by which it is known in India: the Ganga.

Printed and bound in Singapore by C.S. Graphics

Contents

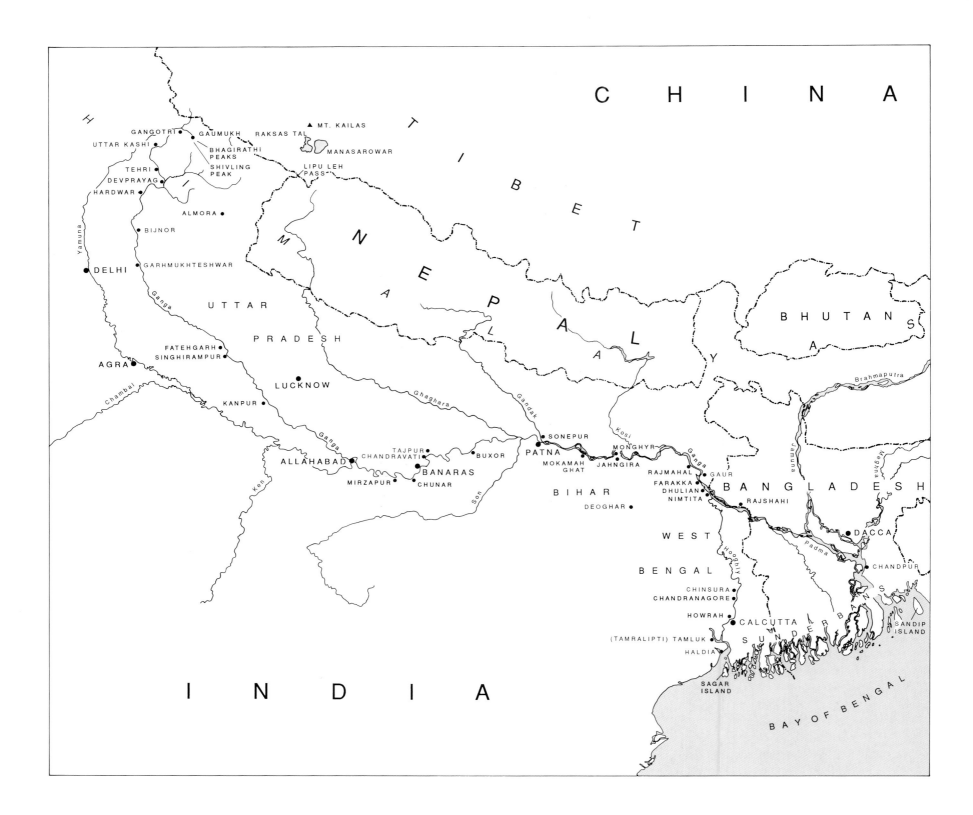

A Long Time on the Ganga

I first saw the Ganga – the Ganges to non-Indians – from the top of the Gola, the granary at Patna, in 1965. Surrounded by a group of villagers, I watched India's most revered river sweep by in a great brown bend past the capital of Bihar state. The Ganga moved me deeply. I had wanted to travel along its 1,550-mile-length since my childhood, when my mother read to me from the *Ramayana*, the epic that speaks so eloquently of the Ganga. My mother also explained the significance of the Ganga as a goddess. She did this not in a didactic way, but casually: while cooking, at meals, or during the many religious ceremonies she performed. For years she herself had intended to make the pilgrimage to the source, but something or other had always prevented her. Finally she fulfilled her lifelong desire. When she returned, after a six-week trek, she was radiant with joy. I still remember her moving descriptions of her beloved Ganga. I remember her account of her first plunge into the river's cold and purifying waters, which left her body numb and her mind transported. Even today, thirty-five years later, a smile lights up her face when she recalls her pilgrimage.

The images evoked by her descriptions of the river were etched in my mind very early on. In time I relived some of her experiences. By 1966 photographing the Ganga had become my passion, a passion which, though it abated in 1974 when I published my first book on the Ganga, revived in 1977 when I returned to the river. I went back again and again until 1990. During this time, I have also answered the captivating call of Lake Manasarowar and Mount Kailas, the *axis mundi* of the Hindu world, from where the mythical Ganga flows as a celestial stream. Five times I have answered the call of the actual source in the Himalayas. I have been entranced by the Ganga breaking into the plains at Hardwar. I have been drawn to the villages of the Gangetic plain: Singhirampur near Fatehgarh town and Tajpur and Chandravati near Banaras. Sometimes, outside a village, a lonely peepul tree shading a few lingams, its roots reaching out to the river, cast its spell on me.

But the crowded cities such as Banaras and Calcutta – and, to a lesser extent, Kanpur and Patna – have also had a strong attraction for me, so much so that I have produced one book on Banaras and two on Calcutta. In Banaras I came to understand the ancient and medieval urbanity of India, sensing in its very air a past peopled with poets and philosophers. In Calcutta, by contrast, I experienced the cosmopolitan nature of a population alive to western philosophy, art and literature without severing ties with the complex culture of the Ganga.

India's own art and history were to be found at countless places on the Ganga. I sensed them particularly at Chunar, from whose sandstone some of the greatest sculptures of the subcontinent have been carved: the Didargunj Yakshi, the Sarnath Teaching Buddha, the Ashokan Lion Capital and others. Chunar awakened in me a sense of history. From the top of the fort, I watched the river make a vast bend. At the foot of the fort lay a part of the Gangetic plain. Standing there, I imagined some of the figures of history who had looked out over the same view: Vikramaditya from ancient India, Sher Shah Suri and Humayun from medieval India, and Warren Hastings from British India.

I witnessed history of a different sort at the *melas*, the festivals. These busy, bustling gatherings drew me into a past which links to the present through the pageantry and practices of India. I went to *mela* after *mela* – at Sonepur, at Hardwar and Allahabad, at Sagar Island and elsewhere. At Sagar Island – in India, but near the Bangladesh border – Hindus believe the Ganga flows into the nether world, the sea, which is inhabited by the *nagas*, the semi-divine water spirits. In Bangladesh, another arm of the Ganga – the Padma – is joined by the majestic Meghna and the broad Brahmaputra. There the Ganga reached out and enfolded me in its enormous liquid arms, just as my mother had drawn me into her arms and painted for me a word-picture of the Ganga flowing through the celestial world, the terrestrial world and the nether world.

The Axis Mundi of the Hindu World

In the ancient world, for all civilizations and cultures, the mountain, the river, the sky, and the sea had a special meaning. They symbolized power and life. They evoked flights of fantasy. They fired the mind, leading it into unknown and untravelled realms, creating new landscapes beyond the earthly frontiers that we know today. So much of the world was yet to be discovered. At that time, several thousands of years ago, the sacred geography of India was conceived, and because India has an unbroken civilization up to the present day, that sacred geography is still a part of the country's living culture.

Our forefathers conceived of Mount Kailas, in Tibet, as the earthly metaphor for the cosmic mountain: Mount Meru, the *axis mundi* of the world and the source of all life-giving waters. Four rivers flowed out from Meru as they do, in actual fact, from Kailas. Mircea Eliade, the great historian of religions, wrote: ''Since the sacred mountain is an *axis mundi* connecting earth and heaven, it in a sense touches heaven and hence marks the highest point in the world; consequently the territory that surrounds it . . . is held to be the highest among countries.''

The ancient Hindus created the *Ilavrita*, the divine enclosure, north of the Himalayas, away from the realm of men, around distant Mount Kailas. In transferring the qualities of Mount Meru to Mount Kailas, they peopled it with divinities, one of whom was the Ganga. The Ganga flows through the paradise of Siva, on Mount Kailas. She is the elder daughter of Himavat, the Himalaya. She emerges from the lake of Manasarowar – literally the Lake of the Mind, because it was born from the mind of Brahma – at the feet of Kailas. Ganga also circles, three times, the heaven of Brahma, on Mount Meru. She flows in a celestial world that represents the peak of spiritual wisdom and knowledge.

Such a world could not have been situated in the banal and flat plain where the ancient Hindus lived their daily lives. It had to be located in a terrain that excited the imagination, that fired the mind, that evoked Mount Meru. Such a land rises abruptly above the scorching and flat plain of the summer. It rises to snowcapped and towering heights. It stuns the mind. It is the Himalaya and beyond it the Trans-Himalaya. It is the Abode of the Gods. Its silence, its bracing air, its mystery, its perennial snows, its forests, its high plain, its cascades and roaring rivers lend themselves to meditation and therefore to knowledge. Beyond the Himalayas, standing stupendously alone, is Kailas, in the Trans-Himalaya. The Ganga is the life-giving link between this heavenly world and the burning plain.

As life developed along the Ganga and her sister streams, temples arose. They were modelled after Kailas. The river and the temple dissolve the boundary between heaven and earth. They help the Hindu secure his release from recurrent birth.

Although the religious iconography of the Buddhist, the Jain and the Tibetan Bon-po world is quite different from the Hindu world, they too give

Kailas the same importance as Hinduism does. All Hindu and Jain temples and Buddhist stupas derive their shape from Mount Meru or Mount Kailas, through the mathematically ordered *mandalas*: the cosmic diagrams with multiple meanings and fixed positions for each deity. The temples and stupas are to the Hindu and Buddhist world what the ziggurats were to Babylon.

At Mount Kailas, the Ganga flows through an unseen and higher reality. Thus the river is an intimate part of the Hindu psyche. It is a rich symbol. It is a life-sustaining metaphor of the complex Hindu world. In ancient times, the metaphorical Ganga was known far and wide. The early Christian fathers called it the Phison, the foremost of the four rivers of Eden.

The life-giving waters of the Ganga nurtured the civilization on the Gangetic plain which developed the epic poems and texts of Hinduism. To understand something of the many layers of the Ganga and its civilization, it was essential for me to make the pilgrimage to Kailas and Manasarowar. During this trying journey thoughts rushed into my mind: was this the pilgrimage that inspired the last scenes in the *Mahabharata*? Yudhishtra has trekked into the mountains. He is being tested. The dog (*Dharma*, the god of moral and religious duty, in disguise) accompanies him. Ultimately, he bathes in the celestial Ganga. He is purified. The epic war of the wounded and earthly plain is behind him.

The mountain, plain and river are the real protagonists and metaphors of India's life, flowing unbroken from the ancient past into the present. The river flows in the realm of heavenly Kailas and the earthly Gangotri glacier. Yet, do we really know from where she comes and where she goes?

The Kailas Pilgrimage

Kailas – Kangrinboqe Feng to Tibetans – is a silvery mountain, rising to 22,028 feet in the Gangdise Range of the Trans-Himalaya. It rises just above the narrow neck of land between the two sacred lakes: Manasarowar and Raksas Tal. Major James Rennell, the Surveyor General of Bengal, in his map of Hindustan (1782), showed Manasarowar as the source of the Ganga but explorers to Tibet would soon separate the sacred and the profane facts of geography.

Since childhood Kailas had been my Shangri-La, but I had pushed the idea of making the pilgrimage to the back of my mind because border skirmishes during the 1962 India-China war had put paid to that possibility. Indeed, I had given up all hope of seeing Kailas when, one day in 1981, I was overjoyed to read a newspaper report that China was once again to allow in pilgrims. People from all religions, all over India, shared my excitement and delight. I know Sikhs, Christians and Muslims who have made the pilgrimage, for Kailas is a throne of culture.

The first pilgrims were divided into three groups. I was in the second group of fifteen. Over sheep trails, past waterfalls and through gorges, we walked from dawn to dusk. For seven days we trekked, up and down, from 3,000 to 17,000 feet. The sweat and the strain drained us. We were often breathless. Rain made walking difficult and cold. Then we crossed the snows of 17,000-foot-high Lipu Leh (pass) into Tibet.

There we travelled on a flat and brown expanse of 15,000 feet. We passed stray farmers and a herd of antelopes. We drove over Gurla pass and then skirted limpid Raksas Tal, the desolate lake adjacent to Manasarowar. Then, rounding a hill, we suddenly came in sight of a majestic expanse of blue, lined on the far side by a snowcapped range of mountains. This was Manasarowar. My heart lifted. The sight was a wordless song, with a slow and sensuous beat. It rose up in me and fed my senses.

Then I turned my eyes towards the north, looking for Kailas. And there it was, the king of mountains, with its tilted crown mocking the world, sitting on the roof of the world, looking down at the Himalayas, looking down at India.

And as I looked up, at Kailas, the song in my heart intensified and touched my deepest sensibilities, because the mountain carried the original cadence and music of the ancient culture of India: it is *the* Hindu temple.

My companions, too, were under a spell. Some of them had rushed to touch their foreheads to the sacred soil and to raise the sacred waters to their lips. A dream had come true. As we drove on, clouds closed in. At the base of Kailas, near the ruins of a monastery destroyed during the Cultural Revolution, some of us camped and waited for the clouds to lift. Others immediately began the circumambulation of Mount Kailas or the *axis mundi*.

On the third day, the clouds cleared. The enormous power of sunlit Kailas pulled me into the lower ranges, on the south side. I kept on climbing, without feeling tired. I think I climbed to over 18,000 feet, until, elated, I faced Kailas, the king.

Then, like clouds, thoughts floated into my mind. What was it about this noble mountain that had inspired millions and millions of Hindus and Buddhists through the centuries? Why Kailas and not Everest? Why did believers and non-believers walk hundreds of miles for a glimpse of it? Why did they face terrifying solitude and even death to set eyes on Kailas? A few years after my visit, three Indians – after seeing Kailas – died in a blizzard that struck as they attempted to cross Lipu Leh, yet the fear of death has never stopped believers or non-believers. Why had it become a divine symbol, so that no man dared set foot on its 22,028-foot-high summit although expedition after expedition had scaled the 29,000-foot-high Everest? I looked up at Kailas. There were the Aryan swastika-like scars on its face, suggesting a smile of silent mystery. The tilt of the crown suggested triumph, a subtle triumph over the lives and the minds of men. The story of that triumph has spread to every corner of India. All of the Hindu world has been uplifted by the mountain's stunning energy.

Yet Kailas troubled me. I could not probe its mysteries with the effortlessness of my fellow pilgrim, Iyappah Karuppanam from Madras. With deep conviction he had told me: "The shape of Kailas is in the form of a Vishwalingam [the lingam of the world and phallic symbol of Siva] as if installed on a *yoni* [the symbol of the female sex – here he refers to Manasarowar]. It is in the stula form; that is, as the divine light. This light is the inner eye. If this inner eye is opened, is revealed, we obtain the ultimate worship of the almighty Siva. The *darshan* [sacred sight] of Kailas is an attempt to find the light of god. This is the holiest, the final and the ultimate truth." Karuppanam saw the mountain as the male form, the lake as the female form, the former representing height and the absorbing power of truth and the latter depth and reflection.

Karuppanam is an orthodox Hindu, a believer. But I am not a believer. I needed some facts or the basics of geography to break through the clouds of myth that surround us Indians. Looking up at Kailas, I saw that it stands remarkably alone. The Tibetan plateau separates it from the Himalayas. From Kailas, the Himalayas appear quite small. I can imagine the ancient Hindus and Buddhists – who loved the dome-shaped Kailas so much that they transferred that shape to their temples – actually believing Kailas to be Mount Meru and rising on a higher plane. From that lofty plane Kailas presides over the actual sources of some of the four great rivers of Asia: the Brahmaputra, the Indus, the Sutlej and the Karnali. And in tradition and myth the Ganga is there too! Until as late as 1807, even geographers, relying on Hindu tradition, placed the source of the Ganga below Kailas.

All the rivers of India are a symbol of the Ganga, including the Brahmaputra and the Indus – which the Aryans first held sacred, later transferring the sacredness to the Ganga. The Indus and the Brahmaputra spread out their arms and enclose the entire Himalayas. They enclose "the measuring rod of the earth", as the poet Kalidas called the Himalayas. These rivers, and a multitude of others, are like veins in the body of India. They carry the powerful pulse of the cosmic mountain, of Siva, of Vishnu and above all of the Ganga, to the tips of the fingers and toes of India: the very ends of the Hindu world.

The Gangotri and Gaumukh Pilgrimage

I had another dream: the trek to the actual source at the Gangotri glacier. When I first tried to go there, as a photographer, it seemed as difficult to reach as Kailas, though this time the barrier was not the Himalayas but India's knotted bureaucracy. The route to the source and the glacier itself is close to the mountain passes on the Tibet-India frontier. At the time photography had been banned well below the district headquarters of Uttar Kashi. But through sheer perseverence, and with the help of a bureaucratic godfather, I ultimately made the trek to the first temple at Gangotri and beyond it to Gaumukh, the Cow's Mouth, as the snout of the glacier is called. I made three treks between 1967 and 1969, chaperoned each time by an intelligence man. On our return, my film was censored. These restrictions were lifted a decade later.

One year I made the trek before the close of winter. The ice-face of the glacier was a region of eternal snow. I was accompanied by my friend Swami Shardanand from Gangotri. When he bathed, he rubbed oil over his entire body and then took a quick plunge into the freezing waters. He came out excited and rejuvenated. On our return trek, as on our journey up, we walked with the Bhagirathi peaks and Shivling looming over us and rising to between 21,000 and 23,000 feet. Below us, the Ganga was a swift, crystalline stream flowing through a majestic blanket of snow, patched here and there by outcroppings of brown rock. Now and then the river would sweep under a snow-bridge and reappear crystal-blue in the sunlight and emerald-green in the shade. It echoed the loveliness and the solitude of Kailas and its sacred lakes.

What Kailas was in the world of mountains, the Ganga was in the realm of rivers: Kailas was far from being the highest mountain and the Ganga far from being the longest river (there are thirty-four rivers longer than the Ganga), yet this modest river had captured the heart and mind of India. Kailas and the Ganga were not awesome; they were certainly not wonders of the world. They related to the human scale of India's life and culture; they allowed human contact. For instance, the mountain and the river (including many sites along the Ganga) allowed the ordinary person to make the *parikrama*, or circumambulation; only an extraordinary person would be able to accomplish such a feat around Everest or the Amazon. In India giant trees are not worshipped. It is the tiny *tulsi*, the basil plant, that is revered. The Ganga is the basil plant, rather than the giant redwood, of rivers.

These thoughts went through my mind as I trekked to Gangotri and Gaumukh during the summer. The river was swift but narrow. It was modest, it was *reachable*, but at the same time it was surrounded by the majesty and mystery of the Himalayas.

I was not much interested in the occasional mountaineers and trekkers whom I passed. They were athletes who scaled mountains. My attention was held by the people of the villages and towns of India, who reminded me of my mother. I watched streams of such men and women, many of them gaunt and haggard, climbing the narrow Himalayan trail, resolutely, step by step, huffing and puffing, stopping to rest and voicing the timeless chant: "*Har, har Ganga* (Hail, hail Ganga)." This chant would bring the reply from other pilgrims: "*Bol Ganga Mai ki Jai* (Say Victory to Mother Ganga)." Then, before they went on, they would look down at the shining ribbon of water hundreds of feet below. The unassuming but majestic sight of the Ganga would restore their spirits, lift their hearts, and relieve some of their tiredness. At other times, when pines or deodars or a bend hid the river, they would look up at a snow-capped peak and that would inspire them. In their naivety, some would ask: "Is that Kailas? Is that the home of Siva? Is that the home of Gangaji?"

Before these people, trekking with little more than belief as their baggage, I felt humbled. My sleeping bag, tent, parka, woollen undergarments, packed food and medicines were a luxury, an act of over-preparation. I could not do without them. I lacked the hardiness and resolution of these men and women who had never walked in the Himalayas before. Many of them had left their villages or districts for the very first time to make this pilgrimage. Now, staff in hand, bundles balanced on their heads, they had set out to realize their lifelong aspiration: to bathe in the Ganga flowing through the Abode of the Gods. Then they would return happily to their homes. And though they might never see the Ganga again, its waters would flow forever through their minds.

But among these were some who would not make it back, who would die at Gangotri, or en route, or on the return journey. But the thought of death did not worry them. They had come prepared, for they considered death by the Ganga to be a blessing. Such a death, they believed, would transport them to the paradise of Siva on Kailas, the celestial home of Ganga. These were also my mother's thoughts when she made her own pilgrimage to the source. But she *had* returned, bringing back urns of sacred Ganga water. When my father died, in 1958, I witnessed the sacred water being touched to his lips.

The Decline of the Himalayan-Ganga

The inspiring pilgrim route to Gangotri had changed dramatically when I revisited it in 1989. The route, a childhood dream fulfilled in adulthood, was no longer a narrow mountain trail. This time I drove all the way to the Gangotri temple. A new and flashy kind of pilgrim had appeared: the upper middle class and the rich who came in speedy Japanese-designed Maruti cars and vans.

There were crowds of noisy pilgrims of all descriptions. Many carried transistor radios and cassette recorders, turned to full volume, playing the brassy and syrupy music of the Bombay films, breaking the spiritual solitude of the valley. The silent, old-style pilgrim was outnumbered. Only a select few walked. Most came by bus. The road had brought the entire Gangetic plain dangerously close to Gangotri; Delhi itself was only twelve hours away by car. The bazaars of India were now well connected to Gangotri. There were more shops, more trekkers, more mountaineers, more pilgrims and more sadhus. To supervise the rush of people the state government had built a police station right above a splendid and sculpturesque waterfall – an act comparable to erecting a Public Works Department building in cement beside the Taj Mahal. The state government proposed to turn Gangotri into a "tourist resort", though where it would find the space in the narrow Ganga valley, no one knew. On hearing the state government's plans, an old sadhu remarked: "We will not permit this place of penance to be crowded with honeymoon huts."

The government had failed to heed the warning of scientists and ecologists: the Himalayan glaciers, which took 5,000 to 15,000 years to form, could disappear within 350 years. A few centuries from now, what will happen to the source of the Ganga? Will the bureaucrats and the bazaars of the plains finish off the glacier? Will the Ganga become one day like the Saraswati, the lost river of India, alive today only in our belief and in ancient literature?

The greatest damage of all was downstream, at Tehri, a small, nondescript town founded in 1818. There a huge dam will be erected, 850 feet high. A drawing of the reservoir showed it shaped like a garupa swallowing the Bhagirathi and letting it out as a long and meandering tail. But though there was a good deal of charm in the project-drawing, there was none at the actual site. I arrived there with the sound of blasting in my ears. Clouds of dust arose, as rock and debris cascaded into a defile. The work on a power tunnel was in full swing.

The dam will be completed, possibly by 1996, providing power, water for irrigation, and drinking water as far as Delhi.

On the Himalayan Ganga and on the Narmada of central India, India's vocal environmentalists have lost their fight to stop the large dams, though it has been established that small dams are overall more beneficial. So the thousands of evacuees from the Tehri site will join the many millions who are the victims of the last forty years of evacuation from five hundred dam sites. Environmentalists warn of the buildup of seismicity since the last earthquake, in 1828. In the event of another earthquake, at least twenty-three villages will be drowned and seventy-six villages flooded. Much of the town of Hardwar will be swept away. The loss of life will be in the thousands.

The fight to stop the dam was lost because of the juggernaut-combination of the plain's politicians and contractors. The benighted Gangetic plain has made its deep inroad into the Bhagirathi valley. But there is some hope at Gangotri itself, because vested interests have little to gain financially. The Himalayan Adventure Trust and the Indian Mountaineering Foundation have joined hands to "save Gangotri". They want to turn the valley into a protected national park. It will be difficult to effect this around a pilgrim route.

But the environmentalists' most difficult task lies in the Gangetic plain, where the sacred Ganga snakes past village after village, town after town, and city after city. In the plain live about one-third of India's 830 million people.

An Encounter with "Faith"

The Ganga flows into the Gangetic plain at Hardwar, which lies at the foot of the Siwalik hills, the last outriders of the Himalayas. To me the town of Hardwar is memorable not because it is one of the seven sacred cities of Hindu India, nor because the Kumbha *mela* is periodically celebrated there. It is memorable because of my moving encounter with a Bihari farmer. Short, stocky, unshaven and dark skinned, he wore a saffron vest and a white dhoti, and when I met him he was engaged in conversation with the *pandas*. These are the ritual-specialists and record-keeping priests, many of whom specialize in fleecing pilgrims. They had just deprived the farmer of most of his money, even though they knew he was about to begin an epic journey. Some time before, the Bihari farmer had vowed that if he became the father of a son he would make a very special pilgrimage. He would carry pots of Ganga water in baskets suspended from a yoke, not by walking, as is usual, but by prostrating his way across Uttar Pradesh and the Bihar states to the Siva temple at Deoghar, near the border of Bengal. During his journey he would be entirely dependent on the goodwill of well-wishers and good Samaritans.

The son was born. He had come to fulfill his vow. A pilgrim to Hardwar had given him Rs40 (£5 in 1967) to begin his journey. He still had this money, wrapped up in a kerchief, when I saw him begin his odyssey. He took one step forward, placed the yoke about six feet in front of him, stepped back, then prostrated, his hands reaching out in a sign of supplication before the pots of Ganga water. He would perform this act again and again, for an estimated five months, until he reached Deoghar.

I have often wondered what happened to him. Did he complete his journey? Did his son receive an education? In my mind the farmer stands as a symbol of all the worship along the Ganga, including that at the great bathing festivals. It is such fervent belief which makes the Ganga a great and sacred waterway.

The farmer had filled his pots of water near Har-ki-pairi, where a footprint impressed in stone is believed to be that of Vishnu. These sacred steps, at Hardwar – the Gate of Hari or Vishnu – are strictly speaking not on the Ganga. The town lies on a canal, just below the point from where it takes off from the Ganga. In 1854 Captain Proby Cautley (later Sir Proby) of the Bengal Engineers built what was then the largest irrigation system in the world. It was a daring project for its time. It cost £2.2 million including the extensions which continued till 1870, and ran for 350 miles, irrigating 1,200,000 acres of the land between the Ganga and the Jamuna, the Doab. The canal ended the major problem of the Doab: famine.

Pollution: the Hydra-headed Monster

Modern India has a different sort of problem on the Ganga: pollution. And it will take much more than daring engineering and Victorian resolve to solve it.

When I first started travelling on the Ganga in 1965, no one in India ever described the river as polluted. Hindus had always seen it as clean, purifying and soothing. The noted savant and sage, Swami Vivekananda, in *Diary of a Traveller*, wrote about being caught in a busy Western metropolis: "I stood in the midst of the swirling traffic and felt restless and disquieted. I drank a few drops of the Ganga water that I carried with me. And all was calm and peaceful again." Even the British travel writer Eric Newby commented positively that the water seemed to have "a genuine capacity for absorbing germs and rendering them innocuous". Today, I would not even drink boiled Ganga water, except in the Himalayas, because of the river's toxic chemical content.

I must confess at this stage that before the late 1970s pollution in the Ganga did not bother me. I did what almost all Indians did, I ignored it. This attitude has now changed dramatically. The Western environmental movement has taken root in India.

But the task of cleaning the Ganga is entirely uphill. At Banaras alone 40,000 bodies are cremated every year. Although electric crematoria have slowly taken hold along the entire river, many bodies are still tossed into the Ganga half-burnt. Dead animals are thrown in without a thought to pollution. Holy men and women, those who die from disease, and rajas are not cremated. After appropriate ceremonies their bodies are tied to large stones and cast into the Ganga.

Yet, the major pollutants are not dead bodies nor the sewage dumped daily into the Ganga, but factories. The Indian Government has yet to prevent the dumping of chemical wastes. There are hundreds of factories on the Ganga, from the antibiotics factory above Hardwar, to the Bata shoe factory below Calcutta. The Calcutta area alone has ninety jute mills and sixty other factories. Between them they pour a massive quantity of untreated waste into the river. All along the river are distilleries, refineries, chemical factories and fertilizer complexes, as well as one atomic complex. Even so, it is not Calcutta that is the major urban pollutant of the Ganga, but the city of Kanpur in Uttar Pradesh. Kanpur has sixty-six industrial units, half the number for the entire state. It is a centre for the infamous tanneries which turn that part of the river, which has little water in it, into a stretch of the River Styx.

The average literacy of the Gangetic plain is 35 percent. The Bihari pilgrim who set out to prostrate his way across the plain was illiterate. He and millions like him could hardly be expected to understand that the average drop of Ganga water contains traces of cyanide, arsenic, lead, zinc, selenium, chromium, mercury, cadmium, phosphorus, nitrogen sulphate and silicate, besides traces of human and animal waste and half-burnt corpses.

The polluted Ganga is, to me, a metaphor for the decline of the entire Gangetic plain. At one time the cities along the Ganga boasted excellent educational institutions. Today the same institutions are ghettos for student *goondas* (street toughs). At the Banaras Hindu University armed police have lived on the campus since the mid-1970s. Simultaneously, there has been a decline in public life and morality. Fundamentalism has risen to alarming proportions. Intercommunal relations survive on the thinnest of artificial threads. The cynical, corrupt and conniving politicians of the plain have used them to turn the rich land of the Ganga into a physical and mental wasteland. Yet, the good and bad of India is to be found in the plain. It is a symbol of India. Here the classical civilization of the Vedas, the Upanishads and the Epics was developed. Here, in this very century, the freedom movement was born. This was a land of poets, priests and philosophers. This is the land from which seven of the eight Prime Ministers of India have been chosen. This is the land which sends an overwhelming number of parliamentarians to New Delhi. This land is a vast vote bank of new post-Independence identities and voices. This land sprawls at the feet of the Himalayas and Kailas. This land of the Ganga, will it revert to even a trace of the higher ideals of India's past?

As one who has followed the Ganga and its many-layered world in mountain, plain and delta, I can only hope that the new voices mature and modernize. Can Indian tradition demand anything less?

Row-boats, Sail-boats and Steamboats

Modernity touched India through the steamship. It was India's early link to the industrial revolution in Europe. Steamboats on the Ganga played a crucial role in the creation of the British Empire and indirectly in the birth of the Bengal renaissance – the foundation of modern India. But before the steamboats there was a vast variety of row-boats and sail-boats on the river. Most of them have disappeared, at least on the Indian side.

There were boats shaped like fish, boats for musical soirées, baggage boats, boats with a variety of cabins. Of the cabin boats, only the Banaras *bajra* survives, though that also will disappear. There were barges, too, some with painted sides and some which, when packed with animals, looked like smaller versions of Noah's ark. With the decline of river transport and the raising of at least fourteen bridges on the river, traditional craft are used only locally.

I count myself lucky to have seen the boats belonging to the Maharaja of Banaras, which suggest the riverine past. From one of them – a barge painted with lotuses – the Maharaja watches the re-enactment of a Krishna story: *Nag Nathiya*. He sits on a silver chair, clothed in the brocade of Banaras. Crowds line the riverbank. Krishna – played by a pre-pubescent (therefore pure) young actor – jumps into the river from a makeshift tree on floats. He emerges from the water, triumphantly playing his flute and standing on the hood of a demon-snake which he has subdued. The snake is made of wood and is pushed by powerful swimmers.

The Maharaja has another barge, usually moored in front of his Ramnagar Fort (across from Banaras). In its cabin is a trapdoor through which the Maharani and other women lower themselves into the Ganga for their daily bath. During the yearly bathing festivals and the Kumbha *melas* at Allahabad, this barge is parked very close to the sacred confluence of the Ganga and Jamuna. A white-turbaned and red-liveried attendant stands guard outside while the women bathe.

The British used country-craft rowed by muscular oarsmen to transport a variety of goods, animals and personnel. Stamp paper, stationery and medical supplies were often dispatched by boat to the various districts. Troops were transported by boat. Civil and military officers used boats to move their baggage. An officer might hire as many as a dozen boats to carry carriages, horses, livestock, carpets, furniture and trunks of personal belongings. He would be accompanied by a retinue of servants and one boat would be used exclusively for cooking. In 1828 a treasury of almost 4 million rupees guarded by a battalion of troops was brought by a flotilla of boats from Agra to Calcutta. In 1829, 356 treasure shipments – mostly land revenue collections – were made through the Ganga and its tributaries.

River transport was necessary but dangerous. Near Bhagalpur, in Bihar, river pirates still survive. There was also the risk of the monsoon and the capricious Ganga. At places, in the summer, the river was dangerously shallow and ran through a maze of sandbars. Calcutta's insurance companies charged an almost identical premium on goods destined for Allahabad, 800 miles upstream, and a British port, 15,000 miles away, via the Cape. Before steamboats ran on the Ganga, the cost of transport was prohibitive but unavoidable. In 1828 the East India Company's directors in London complained bitterly that the total expenditure of the company, of which transport was a major part, exceeded the revenue by 10 million rupees.

Lord William Cavendish Bentinck arrived in Calcutta in 1828 as the new Governor-General, with instructions to economize, which in effect meant modernization through the development of iron steam boats. Ten years earlier, experiments with steam engines had been tried in Calcutta with a makeshift dredger and in 1823 they had been used to ferry passengers. Enthusiastic and cheering Bengalis and Britons had lined the riverbank. In September 1828, the *Hooghly* left Calcutta and reached Allahabad in twenty-three days. When the ironboat passed Banaras the entire city packed the riverfront to witness the event. But more powerful engines and boats with better draught were needed. They were obtained. In 1830 Bentinck himself made the journey. In 1834 he inaugurated the first regular line of steamboats with the *Lord William Bentinck*, equipped with a 60-horsepower Maudsley & Field engine. With a flat in tow, it made the round trip in eighteen days. Now the faraway battlefields could be reached more quickly by river and by road. Thus the Ganga and its steamboats were used – through connecting roads – in the annexation of Sind and Oudh, in 1843 and 1856, respectively; in the conquest of the Punjab in 1845–49; in the Afghan campaigns of 1839–41; and in crushing the revolt of 1857. But in building the Empire, the British also sparked the Bengal renaissance.

India and Europe: an Intense Interaction

The guns for the battle of Plassey were shipped up the Ganga. Down the river went sailingships and then steamships loaded with cotton and silk textiles for Europe. Once British rule settled in, chandeliers, crockery, furniture, cut-glass decanters, European statuary and oil paintings arrived in Calcutta, for the British and the Bengalis. The ships also brought the plays of Shakespeare and Sheridan and Massinger and Molière, the *Iliad* and the *Odyssey*, and Virgil's *Aeneid* – in which he describes armies in waves like the floods of the Ganga. Upstream, through the French at Chandranagore, arrived more provocative fare: the American *Declaration of Independence* and Tom Paine's *The Rights of Man*. The philosophical works of Hobbes, Locke and Rousseau had arrived, along with plans for Palladian buildings. The Scots, a major force in British rule, brought Sir Walter Scott's novels, which would inspire the first Bengali novelists.

In a reverse process the Vedas, the *Mahabharata* and the Bhagavad Gita reached Europe. Possibly the earliest western Indologist was the Frenchman Anquetil Duperron, who earned a living as a soldier at Chandranagore. The greatest British Indologist, Sir William Jones, influenced by Duperron, drew parallels between the Indian and the European classical ages.

Thomas Babington Macaulay, the historian, sailed into Calcutta in the same year as his fellow Utilitarian Lord William Bentinck. Bentinck, as Governor-General, introduced social reforms like the outlawing of sati (the burning of widows on their husband's pyres). Macaulay defeated the designs of the Orientalists and successfully pushed for the study of English.

Neither Bentinck nor Macaulay would have realized their achievements without the support of Raja Rammohun Roy (1772–1833). He strongly championed the abolition of sati after being unsuccessful in stopping the stringent Brahmins from forcing his brother's wife on to the funeral pyre of her husband. He had helped found a college for the dissemination of Western education before Macaulay arrived in India. With a knowledge of languages, literature and religions, and deeply influenced by the monotheistic Upanishads, he founded the Brahmo Samaj (Society of God), a reformist sect. His intellectual lead was followed by notable Bengalis, including the Tagores and Satyajit Ray's family, who became Brahmos. The Brahmos were crucial to the flowering of the Bengal renaissance. Their rationality and morality culminated in the cinema of Satyajit Ray. For him, and for others in the Bengal renaissance, the Ganga has been a subtle theme, a vehicle for this intense interaction.

In the Picturesque Style

Well before Satyajit Ray, the Ganga was an important theme for artists. The early European painters had to travel on the river, that being the route of the Raj. It was a time when the British, consolidating conquest and annexation, began to pay attention to India as a land worth studying and influencing.

The best known of the European painters who came to India are Thomas and William Daniell, uncle and nephew, who arrived in 1786 and stayed until 1794. They and William Hodges, who was patronized by Warren Hastings, left a variety of paintings of the Ganga. Although Hodges made several trips on the river in the 1780s, only one early painter reached anywhere near the river's source. He was James Baillie Fraser (1783–1856), who produced coloured acquatints of his 1815 trek to the Gangotri temple.

These artists painted in the Picturesque style, deeply influenced by the 17th-century European painters: Claude Lorraine, Gaspar Poussin and Jacob van Ruisdael. Edward Lear, who travelled in India much later (1873–75), took this style to its most romantic and dangerous heights.

The painters, many of whom carried the camera obscura, anticipated the arrival of the early photographers. In 1866, Samuel Bourne, aided by a trail of porters, took his cumbersome cameras on the same route as James Fraser, to Gaumukh and the Gangotri glacier. The great Felice Beato arrived in time to photograph the aftermath of the war of 1857. His photographs (of ruins and of the dead) and the work of Bourne (1834–1912) and Linnaeus Tripe (1822–1902) challenged the Picturesque exoticism of the painters. Yet it was these same painters who would touch a deep, lasting and sentimental chord in the later visual art of Indian artists.

The Ganga Sculptures

The painting and photography of the Ganga make up a sizeable body of work. But no visual art about the Ganga matches the charge and bite of classical sculpture. The Ganga and Kailas sculptures were carved between the 5th and the 12th century AD. It was the Muslim conquests which led in the end to their decline.

Somewhat like my journeys to the Ganga itself, I made many journeys to look firsthand at the river's waters chiselled in stone. Near Madras I stood before the descent of the Ganga at Mahabhallipuram. It is carved in a natural fault in a monolithic rock. At the base a cat mimics the worshippers. Elephants arrive at the water. Siva, Indra and Brahma watch Bhagirath in penance. *Nagas,* in prayer, stand in the river. Once, on top of the rock, a cistern full of water provided a symbolic, celestial flow through the fault. This living and monumental sculpture from the 5th century faces the rising sun and the lapping waves of the Bay of Bengal. At dawn the sculpted rock begins to glow. Its colours continue to change with the movement of the sun, until at night it seems like a frieze for the netherworld.

Also in Tamilnadu, at Gangaikondacholapuram, the story of how Bhagirath caused the Ganga to descend to earth was sculpted in the 11th century for the Chola king Rajendra. Siva broke the fearsome fall of Ganga, on Mount Kailas, by catching her waters in his matted locks. From these she flowed in seven sacred streams, one of them being the river Ganga.

The Chola king worshipped the river so much that vessels of Ganga water were brought all the way to southern India to be offered as a tribute to him by defeated rulers. They filled a large water tank, which was known as the "liquid pillar of victory".

While in south India the Ganga is often majestically sculpted, in Calcutta's Indian Museum I saw a more modest representation. Riding her mythical *makara* – the crocodile-like creature – Ganga folds her hands in obeisance to Siva. She is a dutiful bride. Back in the south, Siva's consort Parvati is comforted by him at the prospect of becoming a co-consort.

In Bangladesh, at the Rajshahi Museum, Ganga is not shown with Siva. She is alone and gorgeous. In one of the most remarkable works of Hindu art, an unknown 12th-century sculptor has carved a curvacious and bejewelled Ganga. Though her nose is chipped and her arms broken, the Sena Ganga resonates with the force and finesse of an art that had reached its peak. The Ganga in this sculpture is truly a goddess.

I went westwards, to Udaygiri in central India. There the Jamuna is shown joining the Ganga. I went further west to Elephanta, the island off Bombay. There, in the caves, I saw the Ganga flowing in three realms: the celestial world, the terrestrial world and the nether world.

Still in western India, at Ellora near the city of Aurangabad, Mount Kailas is reborn in the greatest temple art of India, just as it is reborn in the stupa at Borobudur and Angkor Wat. The 8th-century Kailas temple at Ellora was once painted white to be a mirror image of the cosmic mountain. The sculptors must have possessed the same kind of passion as the Bihari farmer, for they have carved straight down one mountainside for one hundred feet. The monolithic sculpture – rather than temple – and its vast pit, the caves on three sides with all their carvings, the giant elephant sculptures and the tall pillars are all hewn from one portion of the hill. In one frieze the three sister streams are depicted: Ganga, Jamuna and Saraswati.

At the base of the main Kailas temple, Ravana, the demon protagonist of the *Ramayana*, is sculpted as a sinewy figure attempting to lift the cosmic mountain. Siva is there too, keeping him down with his big toe. A wall separates the sculpture from the symbolic axis of the temple. Here, too, pilgrims do the circumambulation of the man-made Mount Meru.

Although the entire body of Ganga sculpture is weathered and eroded and has often suffered centuries of neglect and denudation, these sublime works reach deep into our senses and stir us more than any of India's other visual arts. They create a whole world, as if the very waters of the Ganga and the stones of Kailas have been transformed magically into sculpture. They carry us through the panorama of the early centuries of India's ''quest of the mind''. We read that mind through their sculpted stories.

Ancient India gave countless names to the Ganga, among them *Loknadi*, the River of the World. It was the world of the Ganga that Alexander the Great set his heart on conquering, but never reached. It is the river which every Hindu would like to reach. And I, who have reached it again and again, will always go back to it, because it has led me through the whole panorama of India's life and culture, from the age of the Aryans to the age of the atomic power plant. Yet, when I return to it, one day in the future, will it be the *Mahabharata*'s river of blood or the peaceful river of every caste and creed?

1 In the Himalayas

The source of the Ganga has held me captive since childhood. I was beguiled by the idea of a river rising at India's border with Tibet, below majestic mountains, and then flowing into the plains. My childhood was spent in arid Rajasthan, where the Aravalli range reaches no more than a few thousand feet in height. In contrast the Ganga emerges from the snout of the Gangotri glacier at 12,770 feet, at a place called Gaumukh or Cow's Mouth. Above it rise the three Bhagirathi peaks (between 21,000 and 23,000 feet high) and Shivling (21,466 feet high) which are covered with snow all year round. The tales my mother brought back after visiting the Gangotri temple at 10,300 feet and her descriptions of the Ganga's meanderings between towering mountains fired my imagination. After college, when I made the trek, the Ganga's source exerted such a powerful pull that I have visited it five times. The snow, the evergreen trees, the deep gorges, the roaring river and the sadhus (holy men) who live there have been a continuing inspiration to me.

Five sadhus braved the solitude of the severe winter of 1969. Swami Shardanandji was one of them. For twenty years he had lived at Gangotri — three of those years in a wooden shack within sight of the source. Even on our first encounter the South Indian sadhu was friendly. Subsequently, our friendship developed. At Gangotri we took long walks beween leafy pines and cedars, sometimes to Gourikund, where the Ganga cascades over a waterfall and then thunders down a gorge of grey rock. The sight and sound of the river drove away the tiring heat of the plains. When the sky was blue, sadhus would come out of their caves to meditate, in soft sunlight, on the polished white and faded yellow rocks overlooking the waterfall.

Swami Shardanandji loved talking about the Ganga. Like most sadhus, he did not dwell on the days before he put on saffron robes, but he told me he had studied science and engineering in Madras. From his greying beard, frail figure and furrowed face I guessed him to be in his late fifties, but he never disclosed his age.

Otherwise he was frank. He described the few winters he had spent near the source. A family of snow leopards, bharal sheep and Himalayan bears often passed his shack on their way to the river. Alone in the solitude of the Himalayas he had disturbing dreams, dreams of temptation. "But the Ganga came to my rescue. She is my mother; she is my solace. By worshipping her, I conquered my temptation."

Shardanandji introduced me to other sadhus, one of whom was Vishnu-dasji, who lived at Chirbas, a few kilometres from the source of the Ganga. The roof of his crude stone-walled hut was covered with bark and branches of birch trees. The wind whistled through the shelter, perched as it was on the slopes of a lonely ridge. Despite the cold, Vishnudasji remained naked all year round, living on rice, potatoes and lentil curry. When visitors arrived he continued his chanting of Sanskrit hymns in praise of the Ganga and other gods and goddesses. He kept himself warm in winter by staying very close to a fire, and as a result his skin was scabbed and black. I have never again seen his kind of piety.

I was deeply saddened to learn of his tragic death, a few years later, a death brought about by his own generosity. On a summer visit to Tapovan, above the Gangotri glacier whose crevices and moraine he crossed with naked feet, he lent his scanty supply of wood to a group of amateur trekkers who promised to replace it through a porter after returning to Gangotri temple. The porter never reached Vishnudasji. A snowstorm intervened, killing the sadhu.

I have met many sadhus along the Ganga, but those who brave the Himalayan winter near Gaumukh, the snout of the glacier, have my deepest respect. Among them is Swami Hansanandji, or Hansji, a tall, portly and jovial man. In the late 1960s he lived in a two-room stone and tin-roofed hut, with supplies of apples, potatoes, rice, lentils, tea, sugar, powdered milk, wheat flour, spices, sweets, dried fruit and other provisions. Most importantly, the walls of his hut were lined with a winter's supply of wood. A cook attended to his needs. In March 1969, Shardanandji and I, on our way to the source, waited out a three-day snowstorm in the warmth of his hut, enjoying his hospitality. There Shardanandji insisted that Hansji's devotion was no less than that of the austere and naked Vishnudasji, declaring emphatically: "Spirituality is the same on the Himalayan Ganga, at Kailas or in the city."

After 1969 I did not see Gangotri for twelve years. Before I revisited the temple I wrote several times to Shardanandji but there was no response. En route there, I was shocked to learn of his death. I remembered his last letters, sometimes written on the bark of birch trees and enclosing dried petals of the *Brahma kamal*, the Himalayan lotus. They included lengthy descriptions of the Ganga and accounts of his treks above Gangotri to pluck the sacred flowers he sent with them.

Swami Atmaswarupanandji is his *chela*, or protégé. He inherited the sturdy, double storey, four-room log cabin where Shardanandji spent his last years. There he filled me in on his guru's final days. Shardanandji was trekking to

Gangotri after a trip to the plains. He slipped and fell from a narrow mountain path. After he had been carried to the foothills, a doctor advised an operation, but he refused, insisting that he return to his beloved Ganga at Gangotri. But before he could make the journey he died, at Rishikesh, in the headquarters of the Divine Life Society, to which he belonged. His last sigh was: "*Hai Ganga!* (O dearest Ganga!)"

As sadhus are never cremated, Shardanandji's body was placed in a coffin with a few of his possessions, including a lithograph of the goddess Ganga, and the coffin was cast into the swift, clear waters of the mountain Ganga, just before it flows into the flat Gangetic plain.

"Only he who has contemplated the divine in its most awe-inspiring form, who has dared to look into the unveiled face of truth without being overwhelmed or frightened – only such a person will be able to bear the powerful silence and solitude of Kailas and its sacred lakes, and endure the dangers and hardships which are the price one has to pay for being admitted to the divine presence . . ." writes Lama Anagarika Govinda in *The Way of the White Clouds*. This is true also of the sadhus who brave the winter solitude of the upper reaches of the Ganga. I treasure my time among them. I treasure that solitude. The Himalayan solitude, those snow-capped peaks, the youthful and fast-flowing Ganga, the cascades, the firs and pines have often passed like clouds across my mind as I followed the river along its capricious path through the hot and peopled plain.

1   Pilgrims to Mount Kailas at Lipu Leh (pass), Indian side, 1981.

2   *Mansarowar lake, 15,000 feet high, Western Tibet, 1981.*

3   Mount Kailas, 22,028 feet high, Western Tibet, 1981.

4   *A lingam-cairn below the Bhagirathi peaks and Gangotri glacier, 1989.*

5   *Swami Shardanand bathes at the source;*
Gaumukh (Cow's Mouth), 12,770 feet high,
March 1969.

6   *Lalbaba's ashram (hermitage), near the source, 1989.*

7   *A porter naps below the three Bhagirathi*
peaks (21,176 to 22,496 feet high) and
the Gangotri glacier source, 1989.

8   *The waterfall at Gangotri, 1989.*

9   *Student pilgrims at Lalbaba's ashram, Chirbas, 1989.*

10   *A pilgrim cleanses sacred thread, Gaumukh, May 1967.*

11   *The first temple below the source, Gangotri, 1981.*

12   *Lumberman on an inflated buffalo skin, Uttarkashi, 1968.*

13   *Dam project, Tehri, 1989.*

14   *A barber's bench, Devprayag, 1989.*

15   *Pilgrims to Laxmanjhula, 1986.*

2 The Uttar Pradesh Plain

Tajpur, near Banaras, is sited on a high bluff overlooking the Gangetic plain. When I first visited it, in 1970, with a Banaras boatman, its problems did not preoccupy me. I was beguiled by the sight of the earthen oil lamps lining the riverfront and by the spiderweb spread of a fishing net against the setting sun. We did not linger on the riverbank. The boatman took me inside.

We entered the hut of his brother-in-law, who was on his knees facing a niche, in which there was a small and colourful clay image of the goddess Laxmi. Two earthen oil lamps lit up the niche and the bare hut. The Banaras boatman joined the prayers while I watched from a corner. They worshipped in complete and mesmerizing silence. Suddenly the silence was broken by a flat, *thuk*-like sound, as both boatmen's foreheads hit the cowdung floor in unison, as if a powerful force were orchestrating their movements. Their hands and palms were spread out. They were embracing the very earth, the earth of Laxmi. Yet the Goddess of Wealth would remain an illusive figure for Tajpur.

I never forgot Tajpur – its riverfront, its mud huts rising out of the winter mists, its women coming down for water. I returned to it in 1989 when the *Mahabharata* was being televised.

Twenty-seven-year-old Ram Avatar Choudhary could not contain his excitement: "Today Kichak will be killed," he said, "I mustn't miss this episode." We walked through tile-roofed Tajpur set among peepuls and neem trees and clumps of cane, to Chandravati, a stone's throw away. There is no electricity in Tajpur, therefore it has no television. Recently, when the *Ramayana* and the *Mahabharata* were serialized, much of Tajpur went to Chandravati to follow the ancient web of moral tales.

The subject of electrification is very important to Tajpur. All the surrounding villages are electrified. Frail and greying Kashi Nath Tiwari, on his way to plant potatoes, tells me, " The J.E. [Junior Engineer] was given Rs2,600 (£80) for electrification." "Do you have a receipt?" I ask, "No," he replies. He adds: "We cannot complain to the M.L.A. [Member of the Legislative Assembly] because he rarely visits us and he does not care." Yet the electricity lines are only two hundred yards away from Tajpur on the Banaras-Ghazipur road. There, at a tea shop, I met the J.E., who claimed the payment was partial and more had to be paid.

Tajpur has been cheated out of electricity because the five hundred people of the village are in a minority in the constituency. Caste is also an important factor. Tajpur has ten Brahmin and thirty fishermen-boatmen families; in the other villages of the constituency, the Yadavs, the Khatiks and the Pasis are in the majority. Even if Tajpur voted along with the majority its fate would not change, because the M.L.A. would find Tajpur irrelevant to his victory and his needs.

Electrification would bring major changes to Tajpur. Its three wells, today always crowded, could be dispensed with, and water could be pumped up to a storage tank and supplied to each household. Electricity would also mean that more thread could be woven on the *charka*, the Gandhian spinning wheel, by the housewives.

Yet, even without electricity, change has come to Tajpur. In 1972 a lift-canal was completed, connecting to the Ganga. Tajpur happened to be the only place where the river never dried up, so it was there that the lift-pump was installed, pumping water to twenty-four other villages. Previously, hardy crops of maize, millet, jo, jowar and rahar dal (a type of lentil) were grown and watered by the monsoon. Now wheat is the chief crop, as well as rice and potatoes.

In 1970 the main occupation of Tajpur was fishing. Today, pollution has greatly reduced the number of fish in the Ganga. Also, the fine nylon net, introduced in the last ten years, brings in only finger fish and spawn. The traditional cotton net was coarse and caught only big fish: rohu, tangra, gaunch, bam (eel) and gagra. In 1970, half of Tajpur lived on fishing; today there are only four fishermen. In time, they too will abandon the profession.

A few ex-fishermen have opened betel leaf and tea shops. But three former fishermen paid Rs10,000 (£300) each to an agent to fly them to the Middle East. From there, working as labourers, each remits about Rs2,500 (£75) every month to his family. They have been doing this since 1985. I met one of them while he was on a visit home. He was wearing a new pink shirt and carried a transistor radio. He had sent home enough money for his tiled-roofed and mud-walled house to be replaced by a brick building. Another man has left Tajpur permanently to become a rich contractor in Mathra.

Twenty-five former fishermen, now in construction, are dispersed from Bombay to Calcutta. Each sends about Rs225 (£7) to his family. Every day fifteen men bicycle to Banaras from Tajpur to work in construction. Construction work is also better paid than weaving, so eleven local weavers gave up their looms in favour of building and housing work.

Two persons work a loom. In a year they weave ten to twelve silk saris, which they sell, for Rs400 (£12) each, to the Banaras merchants, who price a sari at about Rs4000 (£120).

Chandravati, in contrast, is a prosperous village. In 1970 its two temples were made of bricks and mortar and its houses from mud and tile. Today, 75 percent of the houses are of bricks and mortar. In the village there is 1 colour television set and 29 black and white sets, 2 scooters, 1 motorbike, 2 tractors and 2 taxis. Chandravati was electrified in 1985.

The reasons for the village's electrification and its relative prosperity are obvious. Chandravati boasts two Jain temples which draw many rich pilgrims from all over India. The Jains are a wealthy community. This influential village will now urge the government to take the necessary measures to check the erosion of the Ganga that threatens one temple, overlooking the river. They are also pushing for the riverfront of both villages to be electrified because thousands camp there during two festivals. Will this be a stroke of luck for Tajpur? Or will the J.E. still vacillate?

Soon after visiting Tajpur, in 1989, I went to Allahabad to the Kumbha *mela* festival. Thousands of poles carried electricity lines into the temporary township, reminding me of the J.E.'s words. They sounded surreal: ''For every nine poles, three are free, the rest have to be paid for.''

In the gloom of his hut, Surya Narain, a Tajpur weaver, says wistfully, ''Electricity would make a difference to our lives.''

16   *Ardh-Kumbha* mela *(six-yearly bathing festival), Hardwar, 1968.*

17   *Kumbha* mela *(twelve-yearly bathing festival), Hardwar, 1986.*

*18   Goddess and buffalo,
Garhmukhteshwar, 1968.*

19   *A village near Bijnor, 1989.*

20　*The village school, Singhirampur, 1989.*

21   *Temple and ghats, Mirzapur, 1989.*

22   *Stone lingam and pilgrim, Vindhyachal, 1989.*

23   *Villagers, Singhirampur, 1989.*

24   *Goat herders, Singhirampur, 1989.*

25 *A father and child, with Chunar fort in the background, 1989.*

26 *A fodder seller, Chandravati, 1989.*

27   *A former fisherman, now a construction worker, Tajpur, 1989.*

28   *A farmer ploughing, Singhirampur, 1989.*

29 *Land denuded by tannery waste, Kanpur, 1988.*

30   Dhobis *(washermen), Kanpur, 1988.*

3 Kumbha Mela: The Great Gathering

"At 2.48 am the Sun is in Capricorn and Jupiter in Aries. God's in his heaven, all's right with India," declared the Shankaracharya of Jyotirpith, one of the four heads of Hinduism. A steady drizzle had started an hour before the auspicious time for bathing. By dawn it was a downpour. Although a continuous crowd moved through the cold January night to bathe at the *sangam* (confluence) of the Ganga, the Jamuna and the mythical Saraswati, larger crowds of shivering people stood and waited for the rain to clear. It did not stop. Finally, those who had waited began to move, making a formidable river of faith. Into Ganga's liquid arms wave after wave of pilgrims ran, splashed and fell. To keep their spirits up they filled the air with cries of "*Ganga Mai ki Jai*! (Victory to Mother Ganga!)" There was thunder and lightning. It looked as though the Ganga was being joined by a fourth stream: the devout.

A farmer looked up at the sky and said contentedly: "This is the nectar which is good for the crops." According to legend, the celebration of the Kumbha *mela* came about because of an urn of nectar. The gods and demons decided to churn the primal sea for the marvels hidden in its depths. A mountain was the churning rod and a colossal snake the rope. The gods caught the tail of the serpent and the demons its head. Among the treasures that emerged were the flying horse, the milch cow, the priceless jewel, the magic moon, the celestial chariot, the vibrant lyre, the white elephant, Vishwakarma the divine artisan, Laxmi the Goddess of Wealth and Beauty, and Halahala the deadly poison. More marvels kept appearing until Dhanvantari the divine healer held up the most coveted treasure of all: the *Kumbha*, or urn of nectar, which bestowed immortality. The gods and demons let out cries of pleasure and rushed to seize the urn. In the chaos that ensued the demons captured it. Not to be outdone, the gods resorted to a ruse. Jayanta, son of Indra, the ruler of heaven, disguised himself as a rook and spirited the urn away. He flew over the earth chased by the demons. During the long flight to the safety of paradise, he rested the urn at four places on earth: Prayag and Hardwar on the Ganga, Nasik on the Godavari river and Ujjain on the Sipra river. It is in these four places that the bathing festival is celebrated.

Jayanta's journey took twelve days, so, taking a day for the gods to equal a year for man, the Purna Kumbha (literally, "full urn") is celebrated every twelve years. The festival is rotated so that every three years there is a Purna Kumbha at one of the four places. Smaller festivals are held every six years (Ardh Kumbha: "half urn") and even smaller ones every year. At the Purna Kumbha at Prayag or Allahabad, 20 million people gather during the month-long *mela* and 4 million pilgrims bathe on the most auspicious day.

The first to bathe are the sadhus. Thousands march in procession to the confluence. In January 1989 it did not rain as it had in January 1977. From the vantage point of a police control tower and by wading to the confluence I watched sects of sadhus file past. Many were naked, their hair matted and their bodies smeared with ashes from burnt cowdung. These *nagas* (literally, "nakeds") were an eerie sight in the January mist. To signal the beginning of the bathing, spears were dipped into the swirling waters of the confluence. The leaders of each sect were carried in silver palanquins and chariots. Swords, shields, tridents and banners were brandished. Bells pealed, conch shells sounded and pipes played. Drummers rode on horse-back beating a tattoo. Some sadhus danced and sang. There were shouts of: "*Har, har Ganga!* (Hail, hail Ganga!)"

At each Kumbha, those aspiring to be *nagas* are initiated. The applicant can be from any caste or creed, but he should have lived nine years in the first degree of initiation as a *brachmachari* (one who has renounced earthly pleasures) and he should have fasted for twenty-four hours and then bathed in the Ganga during the Kumbha. Rituals are then performed in tents. The ceremony climaxes when the chief sadhu gives three deadly blows with a stick to the initiate's phallus, to deaden the nerves. In 1989 I saw approximately 300 initiates bathe in the Ganga. In 1966 I had seen about 2000.

The *naga* sadhu is the exotic element of the *mela*, but it is the ordinary pilgrim who gives life and body to the gathering. About 500,000 *kalpvasis* – pilgrims who camp from fifteen to forty-five days to revitalize the inner self – participated in the 1977 Kumbha at Prayag.

The *sangam* at Prayag is an ancient site. Its sanctity goes back to the Aryan arrival of between 1200 and 700 BC, though the first eyewitness account dates from the 7th century AD, when Hiuen Tsang, the Chinese scholar and Buddhist pilgrim, travelled through India. Huien Tsang tells us that half a million people had gathered at Prayag for seventy-five days to participate in the bathing. Among them was the Emperor Harshvardhan, who performed rites and distributed the wealth of his treasury. Also participating were ministers, rajas, chieftains, scholars, philosophers, ascetics, heads of religious sects and beggars. All India was there, just as it is in contemporary Kumbha *melas*.

Prayag or modern Allahabad was also the home of Jawaharlal Nehru, India's first Prime Minister. When Pandit Nehru's wife died in a Swiss sanatorium, he took her ashes to the *sangam* to pay his homage to the Ganga. He writes in his autobiography: ''. . . we carried the precious urn to the swift-flowing Ganga and poured the ashes into the bosom of that noble river. How many of our forebears had she carried thus to the sea, how many of those who follow us will take that last journey in the embrace of her waters?'' Pandit Nehru spoke for many Indians when he recorded in his last will and testament:

My desire to have a handful of my ashes thrown into the Ganga at Allahabad has no religious significance, so far as I am concerned. I have no religious sentiment in the matter. I have been attached to the Ganga and the Jamuna rivers in Allahabad ever since my childhood and, as I have grown older, this attachment has also grown. I have watched their varying moods as the seasons changed, and have often thought of the history and myth and tradition and song and story that have become attached to them through the long ages and become part of their flowing waters. The Ganga, especially, is the river of India, beloved of her people, around which are intertwined her racial memories, her hopes and fears, her songs of triumph, her victories and her defeats. She has been a symbol of India's age-long culture and civilization, ever-changing, ever-flowing and yet ever the same Ganga . . .

No one has summarized better the layers of time, the layers of history and the layers of culture through which the Ganga flows in mountain and plain and past ancient and modern cities.

31   *Women pilgrims, Kumbha mela, Prayag (modern Allahabad), 1977.*

32   *Ardh-Khumbha* mela, *Allahabad, 1972.*

33   *Kumbha* mela, *Allahabad, 1977.*

34   *Barbers and clients, Kumbha* mela, *Allahabad, 1977.*

35   A mahant *(a head sadhu) in a palanquin,*
Allahabad, 1977.

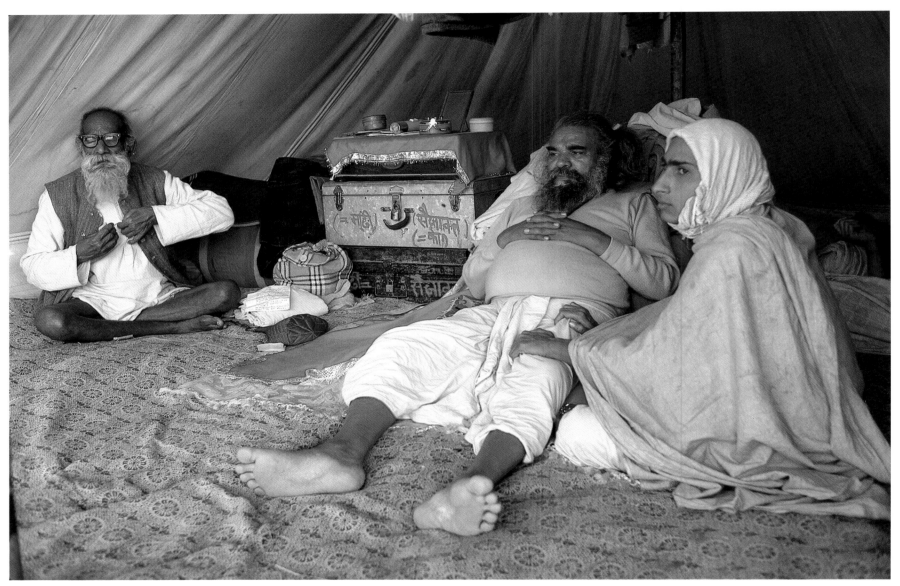

36   *A young sadhu massages his guru, Allahabad, 1977.*

37 *Naked sadhus and their alms, Allahabad, 1977.*

38   *A* mahant *in a chariot, Allahabad, 1989.*

39 *Ash-smeared sadhu and pilgrims, Allahabad, 1989.*

40   *Krishna devotees dancing, Allahabad, 1977.*

41   *Trumpeter and Krishna devotee,*
      Allahabad, 1977.

42   *An attendant holding the sadhu's clothes and mace, Allahabad, 1989.*

43   *A sadhu shouting "Victory to Ganga!", Allahabad, 1989.*

44   *Sadhus in procession, Allahabad, 1989.*

45   *Sadhus plunge into the confluence of Ganga and Jamuna, 1989.*

46   *Pilgrims worshipping Ganga, and rising sun, Allahabad, 1989.*

4 Banaras

Rowing out on the river at Banaras, I am carried by the layers of time, decay, destruction and renewal into the distant ages of India. Yet there are layers that are not easily visible, for instance the rise and fall of Buddhism from the 6th century BC to the 12th century AD. But the advent and inroad of Islam is immediately apparent: the Moghul Emperor Aurangzeb's mosque looms over the river at Panchganga ghat.

For a new religion and a new way of life to establish itself on the river at Banaras meant change and upheaval. Shrewdly, the English raised their settlement not on the crescent-shaped banks at Banaras but at what they called the Civil Lines, at the edge of the city. The Buddha too had chosen to preach at the edge of Banaras, at Sarnath. But the English, unlike the Buddha, brought no challenge to the city's religious philosophy. Their contributions were largely materialistic, technological and educational. In time, these would have a telling effect, but in a most Indian way. For the old city is a buffer between the outside world and the ageless river. It is a maze and filter which transforms every change and challenge, adapting it to the traditional way of life. Witness: when the *Ramayana* was serialized in 1987–88, a television set was installed for public viewing. It was the object of ceremony. Before the Sunday programme began – drawing much of Banaras indoors, from the river and the lanes – a priest raised a brass lamp with lighted wicks and described auspicious circles over the television set. Using vermilion paste he marked the television with the Sanskrit word Om, the cosmic Hindu sound. Only then was the television turned on.

Early on in my twenty-five-year-long association with Banaras, I had concluded that the city was resistant to change. But in time I revised my view. Banaras does allow change, but at its own pace and in its own particular way.

Change has crept up the streets of Banaras from the Civil Lines. The horse carriages, the carts and the bicycle rickshaws are overwhelmed by the speedy, put-putting, three-wheeled motor taxis (autos), the scooters, the mopeds, and the Maruti – a Japanese designed car. Often a god or goddess or both decorate the vehicles, or the word Om may be scrawled in vermilion on the windshield or the dashboard – where the fragrance of incense sticks may merge with exhaust fumes. The macho motorbike has been adopted by the *goondas* (street toughs) as their favourite vehicle.

Dr Rai Anand Krishna, a noted art historian, who taught at Banaras Hindu University (BHU) until 1985, mourns the change wrought by the *goondas*: ''The motor-cycle and scooter-riding *goondas*, with their half-baked education, have cut the BHU's traditional links with the city's now depleted intellectual life. Banaras is adrift.''

Banaras has been celebrated for its intellectual life for thousands of years. The city once housed colonies of ashrams where students apprenticed themselves to gurus to learn the Vedas. The subcontinent's finest philosophers and scholars lived in the ashrams, among them the grammarian Patanjali in the 2nd century BC, the philosopher Shankara in the 8th and 9th centuries AD, the theologian Ramanuja in the 11th century. In this atmosphere of Banarasi learning Tulsi Das (1543–1623) wrote the Hindi version of the *Ramayana*.

The layers of light, the layers of thought and the layers of time in which Banaras is wrapped are best sensed on the riverfront between the Rajghat plateau above the Malaviya bridge and Asi ghat above BHU. The plateau was an Aryan settlement 2,500 years ago. It was the Forest of Bliss, with no temples and statues. Its people worshipped only the elements, but ultimately their religion became ritualized and stagnant. Then the Buddha introduced an alternative to Hinduism.

Both Buddhism and Hinduism flourished until the former began losing ground. The death blow to Buddhism was struck by Qutab-ud-din Aibak in 1194. He razed Kashi, the older city, to the ground. When it was rebuilt, as Banaras, south of today's Malaviya bridge, Buddhism survived mainly at the edge of the city, at Sarnath, where the Buddha had preached his first sermon. Yet the agony of Banaras was not over. Muslim rulers continued to smash Hindu temples and build mosques on those very sites until the 17th century. Today, no building in Banaras is more than 350 years old.

Yet the idea of age is in the very air. On the riverfront it is sensed on the maze of steps that drop sharply or gently to the river and among the crumbling temples and towering palaces raised by princes and merchants. It is also written in the multiplicity of individual rites and rituals that flourish on the river. At Banaras, however, the modern age has finally snaked its way through the maze of narrow lanes, but it is a modernity that has been adapted to the city's needs.

An important change has finally taken place at Harishchandra ghat, one of the town's two cremation sites. Through the ages, the *doms* have traditionally been the guardians of the sacred fire with which the funeral pyre is lit. Every year they cremate approximately forty thousand bodies. Until his death in 1986, Kailasnath Choudhary, their leader, known as the *dom* raja, fought tooth and nail with the bureaucrats residing in the British-built bungalows of the Civil Lines to stop them from introducing an electric crematorium to the city. It was only after his death that the bureaucrats coerced his teenage successor into accepting the electric crematorium. It has now been in operation for three years. A cremation there costs Rs50 (£1.50), while the *doms* charge even the poorest villager Rs500–Rs800 (£14.50–£23.00) for the traditional rite. Naturally, the electric crematorium has caught on. The community of four hundred *doms* is upset; they complain that the electric crematorium violates the rules of the Hindu's last rites. "A son should light his father's funeral pyre," says the young *dom* raja, "How can he do so in the electric furnace, where a stranger pushes a button?"

The Harishchandra ghat crematorium is a crude brick and cement structure raised on pillars, by the Ganga. It could easily be mistaken for an unfinished cinema hall or a crude sort of factory. Inside, it resembles a neat, clean, tiled bakery, except for the bodies waiting to be pushed into the two noisy ovens.

Outside the crematorium I saw a knot of villagers resting against the wall, waiting for the cremation to end, and I asked them what rites they had performed. One of them replied: "We do our rites at home, before and after the cremation." They had turned their back on the *doms*. Yet below the electric crematorium, the traditional pyre burned, pushed into a corner, in the confined space of the ghat. Two doms were busy with it. And bodies lay by the Ganga, waiting to be dipped into the river. Over one of them a man held an oil lamp with a wick, which he circled five times. As I walked away up a lane, I passed eight professional dancers and singers, beating sticks, cymbals and a drum. They had accompanied a group of mourners bringing their dead to the Ganga. They stood outside the Shivam Silk Emporium, which I noticed was less busy than the electric crematorium. I thought how easily Banaras mixes the sacred and the profane. It has had thousands of years of practice in doing so.

47   *A* bajra *boat and summer bathing, Banaras, 1988.*

48   *A Muslim weaver, Dashaswamedh ghat, Banaras, 1988.*

49   *Swimmers, Banaras, 1988.*

50   *Bathers and* Nandi *(Siva's bull) sculpture, Banaras, 1986.*

51   *Wrestlers and sculpture of Bhima (Son of Wind), Ram ghat, 1985.*

52   *Wrestlers on the great sandbank, Banaras, 1985.*

53   *Swimmers and diver, Scindia ghat, Banaras, 1985.*

54   *Bathers, lingam and Siva's bull, Banaras, 1985.*

55　*Priest, woman sweeper and others, Dharbhangha ghat, 1986.*

56   *Holika (the mythical witch) being burnt, a body prepared for cremation and a political poster, Banaras, 1985.*

57   *Image makers and the goddess Durga, Banaras, 1986.*

58   *An image maker's wife and Vishwakarma (god of artisans), 1985.*

59 *A priest at Dharma Kupa (Well of Wisdom),*
Banaras, 1986.

60   *A bride, groom and priest, Banaras, 1988.*

61   *Crowds at Lolarka Shasthi, a fertility festival, 1985.*

5 Bihar

It was in the benighted state of Bihar that I first began photographing the Ganga. In 1965 I arrived in Patna and took the train to Mokamah. I knew about Mokamah ghat from the writings of Jim Corbett, the naturalist and hunter of man-eating tigers. Corbett had contracted to transship goods at Mokamah ghat in 1895. It is a strategic location, between Patna and Monghyr. The rail line to Assam is routed through Mokamah. Before Indian Independence a ferry linked the tracks on both banks of the Ganga. Though a much needed rail and road bridge had been built in the early 1960s, the railway continued to use the riverbank workshop to repair barges and wagons needed elsewhere.

I had arrived at Mokamah ghat with a small assignment to photograph the Ganga, but I did not even get close to the bridge. I took a rickshaw to a spot overlooking the workshop, and stepped out, openly carrying my cameras. Within minutes shouts arose from the railway workmen: "Spy! Spy! Catch the spy!" Photography of the bridge was prohibited. I stood transfixed as two railway policemen ran to grab me. They escorted me to the Mokamah police station, where I learnt that war had just broken out with Pakistan. My assignment letter, mentioning the bridge as a possible subject, was considered to be incriminating, so I was detained at the police station following orders by telephone from Patna police headquarters.

The next morning an intelligence man arrived from Patna. When he saw me, his face fell. "Is this the spy?" he asked. My naive and just-out-of-college appearance obviously suggested otherwise. He then questioned me at length. After he had finished he left in disgust. The Superintendent of Police (the S.P.) then arrived and I was summoned to his car. "Young man, we know you are innocent", he told me, "but the law must take its own course. This is wartime. We cannot take any chances. You will be released after we verify your bona fides from your home town." It took two weeks for the police to establish my identity. In the meantime, I slept on the police station veranda at night and lounged there all day. On my release I returned to Patna.

It was August. I wanted to check out the Sonepur fair held every November. I planned to return when hundreds of elephants, as well as cattle, bullocks and horses, are brought to a two-week market which springs up on the Gandak where it joins the Ganga, across from Patna. Today a bridge connects the two banks of the Ganga but in 1965 paddlewheel ferries – like those made famous by Mark Twain on the Mississippi – transported passengers, goods and animals.

I boarded an overloaded ferry. From time to time these ferries carry many of their passengers to a watery grave. But if there was danger, there was also spectacle. A rainbow arched over country boats with billowing orange sails. I was photographing this scene when an imperious schoolteacher interrupted. His first words: "You are photographing government buildings," drew a knot of passengers around me. The schoolteacher declared my light meter to be a transmitter and my cameras to have a marksmanship of several miles. "You are a spy," he stated angrily. Within minutes, after a "VIP passenger" – a former minister in the state government – had endorsed the schoolteacher's opinion, I was back in custody in the dingy hold near the engine room, under the watchful eye of a guard armed with a pre-World War II rifle. At Sonepur I was handed over to the police at the railway station. Again I was questioned. This time I added my Mokamah experience to my story. The police officer smiled sympathetically when I told him I was a Rajput from Rajasthan. Later, he confided in me that he too was a Rajput. That explained his generous treatment in caste-conscious Bihar.

But by dusk the police had locked themselves in the station with me, after hundreds of people had gathered outside, shouting: ''Give us the spy!'' They dispersed late in the evening after the police assured them that severe action would be taken against me.

From Sonepur the police could not telephone Patna. So in the morning I was escorted to Muzzafarpur, the district headquarters – a few hours away by train. From there the Patna police were informed. The S.P. responded: ''I know the young man, bring him to me.'' In Patna, which took a full day to reach, the S.P. advised me to return to Rajasthan. ''Your experiences could be far worse. You could be beaten up, and your cameras smashed or snatched. We are asking the public to be very vigilant.'' I left. But I went back to Bihar that November.

Even on my first trip I noted Bihar's striking qualities. Although its nastiness got under my skin, I remembered the river, the boats and the astonishing, sweeping view from the top of the Gola, the beehive-like granary at Patna.

From it I could see Pataliputra, the capital city of the Mauryan Empire, whose farthest frontier was Peshawar, at the foot of the Khyber Pass. Megasthenes, the Greek Seleucid ambassador to the Mauryan court (303 BC), wrote of the city: ''The place is adorned with gilded pillars clasped with vines embossed in gold and birds of silver. The palace is open to all comers, even when the king is having his hair combed and dressed.'' He described a city with 64 gateways and 570 towers. Then, over the centuries, Pataliputra lost its greatness and was eventually replaced by Patna, a nondescript town, part of which – Bankipore – was the mundane setting for E.M. Forster's *A Passage to India*.

Even before my arrival in Bihar I was familiar with its extraordinary history. It is part of every school curriculum. I knew that Buddhism and Jainism had been born there. I knew about the Emperor Ashoka renouncing war, converting to Buddhism and spreading the doctrine far and wide. I knew of the Buddhist Jataka tales and Kautilya's *Arthashastra* (similar to Machiavelli's *The Prince*, but more complex). I knew of Sher Shah Suri, who ruled the subcontinent from Sonargaon, near Dacca, to the Indus near Peshawar. I knew that his innovative system of government had been adopted by the Moghul Emperors. I knew the British had established their rule when Hector Munro won at Buxor, Bihar, in 1764. I knew that Mahatma Gandhi had launched the freedom movement at Bihar when he supported the protest against the British indigo planters.

At college, my professor would exclaim: ''What is the history of India, without the history of Bihar?'' But what a contrast the past of Bihar is with the present! Yet I love the state for its history, and for its splendid sites, such as the monastery of Nalanda and the island of Jahngira. I love it for its gatherings, like the elephant market at Sonepur. There, on three visits, I have seen hundreds of elephants. I have seen them as monsoon clouds – the traditional imagery of the sacred elephant in Hindu life and thought, which bestows bounty and represents rain-bearing clouds. The ancient and medieval history of Bihar was like a vast armada of rain-filled clouds, spreading benediction far and wide. Then followed a famine of thought, justice and communal harmony. Such is the painful land through which the Ganga flows.

62   *Woman at Sonepur fair, 1988.*

63   *A bicycle rickshaw driver, Patna, 1987.*

64   *Cosmetics and trinkets salesmen, Buxor, 1989.*

65   *The granary, Patna, 1967.*

66   *A pilgrim to Sonepur fair, 1988.*

67   *Bathers and sand for construction, Patna, 1988.*

68   *A body ready for cremation, a barber and client, Patna, 1988.*

69   *Pilgrims to the Siva temple, island of Jahngira, 1983.*

70   *A truck, boy and goat, Patna, 1988.*

71   *Advertisement for a fan, Patna, 1988.*

72,73   Elephants and pilgrims, Sonepur fair, 1988.

74 *A young mahout killed by his elephant gone* musth, *Sonepur, 1967.*

75   *The river as sculpture, Penance of*
Bhagirath or Arjun, Mahabhalipuram,
Tamilnadu, 1970.

76   *Picnickers at Sanghi Dalan pavilion, Rajmahal fort, 1989.*

6 The Monsoon Rains

In Rajasthan, my homeland, rain is scarce. So when it thundered and poured, all of us children would rush to the rooftops to soak to the very bones in the life-giving monsoon. After three long and sun-scorched months, the rarity of rain made me long for and love the season of showers and breezes. I have never lost my love for the monsoon rains. It is shared by all Indians of all times.

I did not fully comprehend the majesty of the monsoon until I witnessed the fury of the Ganga. The monsoon has two dramatic qualities: its ability to cause widespread destruction and its ability to inspire deep, poetic feelings. Before the monsoon, I had often watched the Ganga dry up into a rivulet, disappearing into vast and blistering expanses of sandbanks in the Gangetic plain. Then in late June the duststorms diminish; clouds float in from the mouth of the Ganga bringing with them the threat of rain. The river is grey; dust and sand swirl around its banks. The clothing of men and women flaps in the wind. Or the wind dies completely. Then suddenly the monsoon breaks. Torrents of rain soak the parched earth. Or it breaks in spurts and stops. The river rises. By August it is often in spate. The current hums with a whirring sound. It sweeps away fields, huts, cattle – anything in its turbulent path.

In Uttar Pradesh, in 1982, 2,000 villages were marooned and 15,000 houses collapsed or were damaged. In such years the Ganga is as wild as when she burst into Siva's locks, intending to sweep the earth away. But on the Gangetic plain there is no Siva to break the Ganga's angry flow.

In Banaras, in 1967, I witnessed the rage of the river. It rose above the ghats — the bathing steps. It rose above temple tops. It made canals out of streets. Houses collapsed. Telegraph poles and trees fell and blocked the waterlogged roads. The river reached half a mile into the town. And yet life went on: the cremation ghats were moved to roof tops. Many shopkeepers attempted to keep their shops open by erecting temporary barriers. The floods obliterated the physical dividing line between commerce and rituals; ablutions were conducted before shopfronts. Such extraordinary floods hit Banaras about once in a decade, but the city is quite prepared for the frenzied river.

I witnessed three kinds of reactions to the floods. There were those people who were not threatened because they lived on the upper floors of buildings; and there were those who were so poor that their few possessions could quickly be moved to safety. Some of the latter slept on narrow platforms in front of shops, others played chess in similar spaces and still others crossed from one house to another in the narrow lanes by using ladders, on which they also lazed. These were novel but temporary platforms. But of course there were those for whom the threat was real. The water had entered their rooms. They struggled to get their belongings out, helped by neighbours and boatmen who had answered their cries. There were shouts and cries from many sides, and students, priests and pilgrims were eager to lend a hand. Yet above the sounds of alarm could be heard the pealing of the temple bells and the chant of the mourners: "*Ram, Ram Sat Hai* (The name of God is truth)."

Banaras, sited on a high bank of the Ganga, knew how to cope with the river's rage: it would wait it out until the waters were placid again. It had centuries of experience of waiting. Through the ages, how many floods had Banaras witnessed? How many calamities?

Although the city's buildings were made of stone, mortar and cement, there were few solid structures in the villages. I was rowed out by four oarsmen to a couple of miles outside Banaras. There I felt and saw the real rage of the Ganga. I saw mud walls collapsing and thatched roofs falling, raising clouds of dust. I saw ants seeking shelter on leaves, snakes entwined on tree trunks, cattle on roof tops. And I saw villagers crowding the few sturdy buildings. While waiting for the floods to subside, the villagers were greatly in need of food. Unlike Banaras, they were cut off. Theirs was the real tragedy. Nevertheless, the belief in the Ganga remained unchanged. "We have to pay for our sins," one villager told me, "The Ganga is angry."

Together with its destructive side, the monsoon is blessed with beauty. Above the muddy waters of the Ganga the sky constantly changes from molten lead to clear azure to an immense armada of fleecy and rain-bursting clouds. Peacocks perch on trees, raising their slender necks to the sky, piercing the air with their shrill calls.

But there are years, 1965 and 1966, for example, when the monsoon fails. Drought and famine prevail. In those two years I travelled extensively in the Gangetic valley. The only water was two hundred feet below the soil, useless without motorized drills and pumps, of which the relief organizations did not have enough. Besides, there were too many villages and too much apathy.

In the village of Basehra, near Allahabad, there was a narrow channel of water, but it was out of reach of the Harijans, who are outside the caste structure and are the poorest, most discriminated against people in India. Between their meagre land and the channel lay the farms of the Thakurs, the warrior caste who ruled the village. One Harijan woman, deeply in debt to the moneylenders, wept and asked: "How can it rain, where one man eats and another doesn't? Can the gods allow rain in such an evil place?" Her husband held up grass and berries, exclaiming: "This is our daily diet."

In spite of its sadness, the monsoon is a season of song, of joy, of festivals and music. The ragas *Desh* and *Megh Malhar* are often sung or played by classical Indian musicians. These racing and sensual ragas please and provoke the senses.

Bol Bom is an unintelligible sound that pleases Siva immensely. It is chanted by pilgrims to the island of Jahngira, off Sultangunj, 131 miles east of Patna. In the Hindu monsoon month of *Shravana* (July–August) saffron-clad pilgrims carry yokes with pots suspended from each end to collect Ganga water at Jahngira, where the Ganga makes a crescent shape and flows north, making this spot sacred. Pilgrims travel by ferry to the island, a pile of shapely rocks housing a temple to Siva and a variety of shrines. There they offer *Gangajal* – Ganga water. Then they walk briskly, or the rare few prostrate their way, to Deoghar, 72 miles away, to another abode of Siva. Fatigue is dispelled by the *Bol Bom* chant. As one voice dies, another takes up the chant so that an intermittent chain of sounds connects Jahngira to Deoghar.

Among the pilgrims are the *dak bams*, who trek without resting, covering the distance in twenty-four hours. This penance is believed to bring the blessings of Siva for happy marriages, for cures for diseases and for a variety of reasons, including success in litigation. The belief is that any wish made at Deogahr is fulfilled. My own wish has been to return often to the Mont St Michel of the Ganga, where the whitewashed temple shines or softens according to the shifting light of the monsoon's mood.

77 *Women caught in monsoon rains,*
Monghyr, Bihar, 1967.

78   *Farmers and herders, near Plassey, 1983.*

79   *Vegetable vendors, Howrah bridge, Calcutta, 1988.*

80,81   *Man dozing, and chess players, Banaras, 1967.*

82   *A man lazes on a ladder,*
     Banaras, 1983.

83   *A woman and children,*
Banaras, 1983.

84   Fishermen and boats, Nimtita, West Bengal, 1983.

85   *Collecting water for Deoghar from the foreshore at Jahngira, Bihar, 1967.*

86   Pilgrims to Jahngira, who will trek to Deoghar, 1983.

87   *Prayers during floods, Banaras, 1983.*

88   Boatmen, near Rajmahal, 1989.

89   *Fishing for hilsa, Nimtita, West Bengal, 1970.*

90 *A villager's belongings stored in a tree during floods near Banaras, 1967.*

91   *Ricefields and lotus flowers, Sunderbans, 1989.*

7 West Bengal

I stood on the ruins of the ramparts of Rajmahal fort. It was from here that Raja Man Singh, the Moghul general, governed Bengal in the age of Akbar. Above the crumbling walls stands a graceful marble pavilion on the high bank of the Ganga.

As a child, I had often heard the song about Raja Man carrying the Devi (the Great Goddess) from Bengal to Rajasthan. At Rajmahal that song was going through my mind as I watched the waves of the Ganga touching the base of the pavilion. I thought of arid Rajasthan and lush Bengal's deep fascination with the Goddess. But in Bengal the belief in the Great Goddess is stronger because the land is a gift of the Ganga herself.

The river in Bengal is a river of blight and benediction. Through countless millennia the Ganga has, in its passage to the sea, deposited silt and formed a vast delta. On this fertile loam the life and lore of Bengal has developed and flourished, with a fervent belief in the Ganga and her sister goddesses: Durga, Laxmi, Kali, Saraswati and others – each a personification of the Great Goddess.

The role of the river at Rajmahal (today just within Bihar, with Bengal beginning across the river) reveals its most important characteristic as life-giver and life-destroyer. Rajmahal was a flourishing port until the late 17th century, when the Ganga's deeper channel moved three miles eastwards, whereupon the rulers and traders set up the capital in Dacca, almost two hundred miles away. Some time later, the Ganga returned to Rajmahal and the city sprang back to life, but in 1863 the river again shifted eastwards and again the city was abandoned. In 1880 the river returned once more to Rajmahal, but by then — as a result of the arrival of the European traders — more prosperous ports had sprung up downstream.

I went to Gaur and saw that the ruins of a whole city of mosques, palaces, pavilions and gateways spoke of a similar fate. Gaur was famous before the Ganga changed course in 1575. "It was the most magnificent city in India," wrote W.W. Hunter in *Annals of Rural Bengal* (1897), "In one year, it was humbled to the dust, and now it is the abode only of tigers and monkeys." Even further back in history, an identical fate was met by fabled Tamralipta, on the Rupnarayan river, a tributary of the estuarine Ganga. In the 8th century the port silted up. As a result the very name of one-thousand-year-old Tamralipta was washed away from the minds of Chinese, Greeks, Romans and other mariners. It was not the only port to suffer from the Ganga's capricious meanderings.

From the birth of Hinduism, the Bhagirathi-Hooghly carried the major flow of water, and therefore the lore and legends of Hinduism. Even though, by the end of the 16th century, the Padma had become the major arm of the river, the depleted Bhagirathi-Hooghly still retained the religious ethos.

On the Bhagirathi, at Nimtita, someone told me this Bengali saying: "To live along the Ganga is to live with anxiety the year round." Nimtita is a village just above Dhulian where the Ganga splits into Bangladesh's Padma and India's Bhagirathi. It is dominated by the ruins of the *rajbari* (mansion) of the Chaudhurys, the former landlord barons of this part of Bengal. Robi Narain

Chaudhury told me: "In 1943 a lawn, a garden and a mango orchard lay between our house and the river. In two years the Ganga carried away the entire orchard of 250 acres. In 1958, eight-foot-high wild grass grew along the river bank, stopping the river's erosion. When the villagers cut the grass and cultivated the land, the erosion began. Within two years the Ganga had reached within ten feet of our *rajbari*. There it remains."

Some of the inhabitants of Nimtita see the rooftop statue of a European woman with an upraised arm as that of an angel which attracts the eroding river. They would like to have the statue pulled down, but the Chaudhurys have refused.

In 1943, when the erosion stopped after a year, prayers were performed at Nimtita, on the day of the Ganga Dussereh. To the furious beat of a dozen drummers, a gold lamp was offered to the river. Today, prayers are still performed but with offerings of fruit and flowers, and with a lone drummer beating on the *dhak* drum. Likewise, throughout Bengal, prayers are performed, and festivals held, all year round to many personifications of the Great Goddess. The prayers are addressed to all her powers of preservation and benediction. The greatest of these festivals is celebrated in Calcutta.

By July, as the river rolls in monsoon fury, preparations are underway at Kumartuli and other Calcutta neighbourhoods. Craftsmen busy themselves sculpting images of Durga under tin and tarpaulin roofs. When the rains end the sculptures are ready to be painted. Made from clay, pith and coloured foils mounted on a bamboo framework, the painted sculptures are carried to homes, streetcorners and parks. The worship takes place at fever pitch to the peal of bells, the beat of drums, the burning of incense and the intense fervour of trance dances. Some Bengalis, of course, do not participate in these ceremonies; they prefer to stay at home reading some of the hundreds of special festival publications of prose and poetry. But on the tenth day, Calcuttans crowd the riverbanks as image after image is immersed from afternoon until late into the night.

For the makers of the images, the cycle continues after Durga puja. There is Laxmi, then Kali, then Jagdhatri and so on until the months move on and a series of goddesses have been worshipped and immersed in the Ganga.

In the monsoon of 1690, when the images of Durga were being sculpted at Kalikatta and two other adjacent villages on the Hooghly, a seasoned English trader and Bengal hand, Job Charnock, dropped anchor and founded Calcutta. He chose the site carefully as a trading post. Upstream Moghul extortions and the Nawab of Bengal had made trade difficult for the Dutch, the Portuguese and the French. Charnock's strategic site was close to the sea and well protected by malarial marshes and swamps. The only naturally unprotected front was the river, but there English men-of-war could observe the movement of Moghul troops. In time Charnock's trading post grew into a metropolis.

It is fashionable today to call Calcutta a dying city. But what is true is that Calcutta port has been silting up ever since the main flow of water was carried by the Padma. Had Calcutta been a medieval or ancient port, like Rajmahal, Gaur and Tamralipta, it too would have been dead a long time ago. But in the twentieth century, ports and cities can be kept alive through an intravenous feeding system; the system's components in West Bengal are: the Haldia port for big ships downstream of Calcutta, the Farraka barrage upstream of the city, which ensures a supply of water into the Hooghly, the air cargo containers, the goods trains, the truck traffic and the river dredgers. Yet Calcutta dies a metaphorical death every day, when the power supply is cut for hours. For this reason West Bengal's industry has a feeble heartbeat.

The small trading populations of Rajmahal, Gaur and Tamralipta migrated and set up new port sites, but where will even a fraction of Calcutta's twelve million people go? There is no room even for wonder.

92   *Women bathing near Malda and Gaur, 1989.*

93   A European statue, the Chaudhuri mansion,
Nimtita, 1968.

94   *College students pass the Nawab's Palace, Murshidabad, 1983.*

95   *The Bandel church to Our Lady of Happy Voyage, Hooghly, 1989.*

96 *The view from the Imambara, Chinsura, 1989.*

97   *A Siva image and a cow, Calcutta, 1988.*

98   *Railway line and riverfront, Calcutta, 1988.*

99   *A man coated in clay before bathing,*
Calcutta, 1970.

100   *Sitalmata (the smallpox goddess), and stone lingams being worshipped, Calcutta, 1988.*

101 *A bridegroom and party, from the Marwari community, Calcutta, 1968.*

102   *The Rani Rashomoni household Durga being immersed, Calcutta, 1970.*

103   *The Netaji Subhas (formerly King George's) docks, Calcutta, 1987.*

104   *Fishermen pass the new Howrah bridge, Calcutta, 1988.*

105   *Rush hour, Howrah bridge, Calcutta, 1987.*

106   *Bathers and an old Durga image, Calcutta, 1988.*

107   *A ferry boatman and the sinking* Ratnashobna, *1967.*

8 *The Delta:*
Sagar Island and Bangladesh

When I first visited Sagar (Sea) Island during the mid-January *mela*, my mind was focused on the crowds of pilgrims to the shore-front temple. It was not until a later visit that I noticed that the makeshift temple had been pushed back by the eroding sea. Here the soil was once held firm by mangrove swamps. It was tiger terrain. Three hundred years ago the Sunderbans, the shrubby and saline jungle, reached Calcutta. Now it merely lines the southern borders of India and Bangladesh. The pressure of population has destroyed the forest on Sagar and on the other large islands at the mouth of the Ganga.

The Sagar Islanders boast a 70 percent literacy, yet the majority are poor fishermen and farmers. The latter are noted for growing delicious watermelons, as well as rice, betel leaf, vegetables and chillies. During high tide they use saline water which does no harm to the crops. For drinking, rain water is collected and stored. Life is hard, but the yearly *mela*, when the population of 120,000 swells to 500,000 or more, boosts the islander's income as huts and stalls are constructed and shops spring up to service the crowds of pilgrims.

I am comfortable in crowds. After attending many Kumbha *melas* the Sagar gathering seems a small affair. It was easy to push through packs of pilgrims to the tin-roofed temple of the fiery-eyed sage Kapil Muni, who reduced the sixty thousand sons of Raja Bhagirath to ashes when they disturbed his deep meditation. The Ganga had been brought to earth, through the penance of Bhagirath, to redeem the souls of his sons. The temple honours Kapil Muni, and in the vermilion smeared statue, the sculptor has shown the fiery gaze so famous in legend. Smaller statues of Ganga and Bhagirath flank the sage, and before all three are piles of coconuts, leaf cups with a variety of offerings, and garlands of marigolds, thrown by pilgrims. Periodically, the sadhu attendants ducked forward to push the piles of offerings away.

The colourful *mela* is a magnet for a variety of mendicants and sadhus, besides pilgrims. Among them are the nagas – the naked sadhus – some sad-eyed, some imitating the gaze of Kapil Muni and still others with smiles sweeping their faces. They sit in stalls built by the islanders. There I heard the story of twenty-year-old Sourav Debnath. He had run away from home in Burdwan, West Bengal, while his engineer father was employed in Iraq, and remained untraced for many years until a relative spotted him at Sagar. The following year, the parents came in search of their son. They found him as Mahanta Chandragiri, coated from head to foot in ash and puffing away at a clay pipe. Between puffs of hashish he ignored his parents. They were also rebuffed by other sadhus, until their cry for help was heard by Himalaya Giri, the guru of Chandragiri's sect, who tried to coax the boy back into the custody of his parents. The boy resisted, arguing: ''Why do you push me into returning to a material life? I am not an ordinary person, I possess extraordinary powers of meditation.'' But the guru's powers of persuasion prevailed. The sullen boy was made to wash away his ashes and return with his joyous parents.

Where the boy had washed, Hindus believe the Ganga fills the ocean. There jewels were once thrown as offerings and children were sacrificed to the mighty river. In the morning I saw marigolds being flung into the water and coins being offered. Later I watched islanders groping for the coins in the muddy waters, as pilgrims followed priests in the prayer to the seven sacred rivers. At dusk I watched oil lamps being floated.

As I gazed out at older pilgrims raising the sacred waters to the rising sun and floating the oil lamps, I thought of my mother. She had never been a pilgrim to Sagar. But it was she who by her descriptions had sown the seeds of my passion. At that very moment, she was in a train speeding to the Kumbha *mela* at Ujjain. But my journey did not end at Sagar, as it does for devout Hindus. I went beyond, into the vast world of Bangladesh waters.

I flew into Dacca. One of my first acts was to hire a boat at Sadar ghat, near Dacca. The launch, about fifty feet long, was narrow and crude. In the small cabin were wooden benches. I slept between them on the floor. The deck was just large enough for two deck chairs and the anchor. When the engine was started the boat was shaken by spasms and vibrations. It made me apprehensive, as I had never been to sea before in such a fragile craft. But the big-bellied, betelnut-chewing Bengali master laughingly assured me that the season was on our side and that the sea would be as placid as a lake. After we stocked supplies including a week's drinking water, we sputtered into the Burhi Ganga. The river was a showcase of every century of boatcraft: primitive canoes, cargo boats, sailboats, paddlewheel steamers, ships and launches of all sizes and kinds. Almost every vessel was packed, with people or with sacks of rice and cement, barrels of oil, piles of bricks, or mounds of jute. By the time we had passed the meeting point of the Meghna with the Padma, above Chandpur, I was under the poetic spell of Bangladesh's river life. My journey had become an adventure into an enchanted and unknown world.

There was so much water around Chandpur that the town appeared to be floating. Much of its nondescript and weatherbeaten housing barely rose fifty feet above the water. The faded yellow and brown brick buildings wore an air of fragility. But the tin-roofed jetties for steamers were sturdily built. I remember the railway behind the jetties clearly because I stumbled and fell when crossing the tracks. On one side was the whistle of the train and the sound of shunting, on the other the putter of motor launches, the splash of paddlewheel steamers and the silence of sailboat after sailboat coming in or going out. It is a junction town. I was mesmerized. Among the sailboats was one with a prow shaped like a *makara*, the crocodile-like composite creature of myth and reality on which the Ganga rides. It is not only her vehicle, it is also a symbol of power. In ancient and medieval wars, the *makara* was embossed on swords and shields. I had seen the embossed arms in museums. At Chandpur the *makara*-shaped boat glided in. The boatmen were Hindus, a minority community in a land of about 100 million Muslims. Many boats belonging to Muslim owners also bore images, mainly of mosques or of the Taj Mahal; some displayed Arabic calligraphy. Yet among all the boats and ships, it is the *makara*-prow boat that magically sails in my mind. It moves on a childhood track established by my mother, when she first told me about the *makara*.

The reality beyond Chandpur was water and more water. The Padma portion of the Ganga and the Brahmaputra had embraced and become one. The Brahmaputra is considered a *nad*, one of the few male rivers, while the Ganga is, like most other rivers, female. The waters of these two rivers are so expansive that, flowing as one, they attest to the power of life and death that rivers hold over men and women.

I saw that awesome power on the last islands, where whole populations had been swept away, to be replaced by new and unsure inhabitants. There, at the mouth, I fully realized the mystery and power of the Ganga and why it is a river of legend and a perennial source of song and story.

108   *A pilgrim bows to a sadhu who habitually stands on one leg, Sagar Island, 1985.*

109   *Sculptures of Kapil Muni, Ganga (far left) and Bhagirath (partly visible), Sagar, 1985.*

110   A mendicant and pilgrims, Sagar, 1985.

111   *The Ganga on her vehicle the* makara *(a mythical creature), Sagar, 1985.*

112   Women pilgrims, Sagar, 1985.

113   *Naga (naked) sadhus, Sagar, 1985.*

114   *As pilgrims pray, islanders search for coins, Sagar, 1985.*

115   *Pilgrims to the Sagar* mela, 1985.

116   *A pink Taj Mahal painted on a cargo vessel, Sadar ghat, 1987.*

117 *Hindu boatmen and* makara-*prow boat,
Chandpur, Bangladesh, 1987.*

118   *A ship on the river painted on a truck,*
Bangladesh, 1987.

119   *Mangrove forests and creeks, Sunderbans, West Bengal, 1989.*

120   *Exercising on a launch, near Chandpur, 1987.*

121   *Cargo boats, Chandpur, 1987.*

122   *Sail and ferry boats, Bangladesh delta, 1987.*

123   *A boatman prays to Mecca, near Char Island, 1987.*